Wicked Little Letters
Film Review

"Unveiling the Secrets of 'Wicked Little Letters': Exploring 1920s Sussex

Reymond Wright

Copyright

Table of Contents

Introduction

Title: An Overview of "Wicked Little Letters" There are stories in history that evoke strong feelings in people, scandals that have a lasting impact on society, and narratives that fascinate the imagination. "Wicked Little Letters" is one such story a gripping portrayal of a little-known episode in the history of 1920s England, in which a startling exchange of poison-pen letters demolish the prim façade of a quaint Sussex town. "Wicked Little Letters" opens with a collection of scenes that set the tone for a story full of mystery and dark comedy. Viewers are taken back in time to a time when letter-writing was more than just a tool for communication it was a window into the very soul of society, set against the lovely background of the English countryside. The actual brilliance of the picture unfolds within this painstakingly reconstructed society, where secrets hide behind every closed door, rumors circulate like wildfire, and words have the power to influence the hearts and minds of both men and women. The character of Edith, played to perfection by Olivia Colman, is at the center of the narrative. Edith is a community pillar and the picture of respectability; she is a prim and respectable spinster whose peaceful life is turned upside down when a startlingly offensive string of letters arrives. Colman's portrayal, which captures the essence of a woman caught in the crossfire of controversy and suspicion, is nothing short of captivating. As Edith struggles to understand the meaning of the anonymous letters, her formerly serene existence is flipped upside down with every letter she receives. Jessie Buckley's Rose, a neighbor whose boisterous manner and colorful vocabulary make her a prime suspect in the eyes of the townspeople, stands opposite Colman's Edith. Rose is portrayed by Buckley in a masterful way, giving her a fiery independence and attitude that contrasts with her beauty. Rose finds herself entangled in a web of suspicion and intrigue as the story progresses, her destiny irrevocably linked to Edith's as they negotiate the perilous waters of small-town rumors and betrayal. The exact identity of the letter writer is still a mystery, but "Wicked Little Letters" explores themes of patriarchy, repression, and the destructive power of gossip and rumors as it digs deeper into society's dark corners. The film asks audiences to consider the age-old question of who is truly innocent and who is capable of the most horrific atrocities through excellent storytelling and expertly written dialogue. In creating the opening of "Wicked Little Letters," the filmmakers have built a world that is both recognizable and incredibly alluring: one in which many misdeeds are concealed beneath the surface of respectability and where the power of words can be both a blessing and a punishment. Viewers are attracted into a world where nothing is as it seems and where the truth is waiting to be discovered just under the surface, setting the stage for a narrative of mystery and intrigue.

Chapter 1.

The Cast: Olivia Colman, Jessie Buckley, Anjana Vasan, Timothy Spall

Title: "Wicked Little Letters" Cast. In the world of film, a movie's ability to succeed frequently depends on the skill and charm of its actors. "Wicked Little Letters" is no different, featuring a cast of exceptional actors who imbue their characters with richness, complexity, and genuineness. Every member of the ensemble, from the legendary Olivia Colman to the vibrant Jessie Buckley, adds something special to the film's diverse cast, transforming it from a simple period drama into an engrossing investigation of human nature and society. Olivia Colman: A Display of Superb Acting Leading the group is actress Olivia Colman, a formidable presence in the performing industry. Colman gives Edith a prim and respectable spinster whose world is flipped upside down by a series of disturbing letters life with her perfect timing, emotional depth, and chameleon-like ability to portray a wide range of characters. Colman's portrayal, which captures the quiet courage and tenderness of a woman coping with scandal and suspicion, is a masterclass in subtlety and complexity. Her portrayal transports viewers into the inner anguish of a character trapped in the path of malevolent intent, in a way that is both heartbreaking and compelling. Jessie Buckley: A Rawly Emotional and Fierce Presence Jessie Buckley, a budding star with unbounded promise, is standing opposite Colman. Buckley gives an absolutely riveting performance as Rose, a neighbor whose colorful vocabulary and bold manner make her a prime suspect in the eyes of the townspeople. Buckley draws attention to herself in every scene she is in thanks to her unadulterated emotion, fiery independence, and captivating screen presence. Whether exchanging jabs with Colman's Edith or negotiating the perilous seas of small-town rumors, Buckley gives the part nuance and complexity while also lending it a real feeling of urgency and sincerity. Anjana Vasan: A Powerful Depiction of Willpower and Resolve Anjana Vasan shines in the character of Gladys Moss, the county's lone female police officer, showing courage and tenacity in a society dominated by men. Vasan gives the character depth and complexity by virtue of her steely resolve, quick wit, and unshakable dedication to justice. She also instills a quiet nobility and grace in her. Vasan's portrayal of Gladys serves as a moving reminder of the human spirit's resiliency and the strength of tenacity in the face of hardship as she negotiates the difficulties of law enforcement in a patriarchal environment. Timothy Spall: An Expert in Subtlety and Nuance Timothy Spall completes the ensemble with an astonishingly realistic depiction of Edith's controlling father, Edward Swan. Spall lends a depth and complexity to the role that defies his appearance with his calm menace, subdued passion, and astute understanding of human nature. Spall plays the part with subtlety and nuance, creating a remarkable and disturbing performance as Edward battles his own issues and attempts to keep control over his daughter's life. Colman, Buckley, Vasan, and Spall work together to create the framework of "Wicked Little Letters," giving the movie a depth and richness that goes beyond the boundaries of its genre. These talented performers bring their characters to life with their flawless performances, taking the audience on a journey through a world where secrets are kept behind closed doors and the reality is never quite what it seems. The cast's exceptional talent and dedication to their craft assure that "Wicked Little Letters" will leave a lasting impression on spectators for years to come, as the plot progresses and the mysteries of the past are revealed.

Chapter 2.

Overview of the Film's Setting: 1920s Sussex

Title: An Overview of the Sussex Setting in the 1920s A movie's environment does more than just provide a background; it becomes a character unto itself, affecting the characters and molding the story while engrossing the viewer in an unfamiliar yet fascinating universe. In "Wicked Little Letters," the filmmakers take audiences to the picturesque Sussex countryside of the 1920s a period and place rich in history but on the verge of significant change. The plot develops against this vividly imagined background, creating a tapestry of mystery, controversy, and human drama that enthralls viewers and takes them to a bygone era. England's Rural Charms: Their Quiet Charm "Wicked Little Letters" is set against the scenic backdrop of Sussex, a county known for its undying appeal, charming villages, and gently sloping hills. A sense of peace and tranquility permeates Sussex, from the thatched cottages tucked away among lush meadows to the meandering country lanes bordered by old hedgerows. However, behind the surface, there are simmering tensions. The plot takes root in this distinctly English environment, transporting viewers to a place where people live slowly, behave elegantly, and have strong ties to their communities. The Charm of Country Living The idea of small-town life a world unto itself where everyone knows everyone else's business and gossip spreads like wildfire is fundamental to the setting of the movie. Reputations are carefully guarded and social hierarchies strictly enforced in Sussex's small villages and market towns. In this world, secrets are hidden under an air of respectability and controversy is discussed in whispers behind closed doors. The protagonists in "Wicked Little Letters" negotiate the perilous seas of social expectation, forming alliances and betraying loyalties in their quest for truth and forgiveness against this background of whispered talks and knowing glances. The Great War's Haunting Shadow The Great War looms huge over Sussex's countryside and casts a lasting shadow over the lives of its residents as the film progresses. The wounds from loss and sadness are long to heal, and the scars from the battle are still visible today. The protagonists in "Wicked Little Letters" struggle with the legacy of the past against this backdrop of societal upheaval and collective trauma, trying to make sense of a world permanently altered by conflict and strife. In this world, which is prone to controversy and intrigue, the old certainties have crumbled and the future is uncertain. The Glamour of a Bygone Age "Wicked Little Letters" is essentially a love letter to a bygone period, one of sophistication and elegance, of garden parties and tea parties, of flapper gowns and jazz music. The filmmakers take audiences back in time to a moment of innocence and optimism, when anything seemed possible and the promise of tomorrow loomed on the horizon, through painstaking attention to detail and moving cinematography. Even now, audiences are still enthralled and motivated by this nostalgic and yearning world, which only lives in their memories and imagination. With "Wicked Little Letters," the filmmakers have constructed a world a real, breathing canvas on which the drama of human existence plays out rather than merely a setting for the plot. They enable viewers to travel back in time and experience the wonder of 1920s Sussex a world of charm, mystery, and limitless possibilities through their painstaking attention to detail and captivating storytelling. The universe of "Wicked Little Letters" is the ideal backdrop for a story of scandal and redemption as the plot develops and the mysteries of the past are solved. It's a place where the past is never fully forgotten and the secrets of the present are bound to be discovered.

Chapter 3.

The Phenomenon of Poison-Pen Letters

Title: The Poison-Pen Letter Phenomenon Few historical occurrences have captivated the public's attention quite like the poison-pen letter a go-to tool for someone looking to cause trouble from the shadows and sow distrust and strife with a single penstroke. Poison-pen letters have caused havoc wherever they have been found, from the salons of Victorian England to the quiet towns of rural America. They have left their recipients traumatized and their societies in disarray. The filmmakers of "Wicked Little Letters," delving into the psychology of the poison-pen letter and its enduring effects on its recipients, shed light on this sinister and fascinating facet of human nature. A Poison-Pen Letter's Anatomy A poison-pen letter is essentially an anonymous letter intended to cause emotional distress to the recipient. These letters, which are frequently rife with hate speech, defamation, and flat-out lies, are meant to destabilize the recipient by damaging their reputation and lowering their status in the community. The poison-pen letters that Edith, the main character of "Wicked Little Letters," receives are appalling in their vulgarity and language that is meant to both shock and offend. The real impact of the poison-pen letter, however, is not found in its contents, but rather in its anonymity the understanding that the writer lives in the shadows and is immune to punishment or legal action as the movie makes clear. The Poison-Pen Writer's Psychology What makes someone write a letter using a poison pen? In "Wicked Little Letters," the protagonists struggle with the mystery surrounding the letters' origins, and this is the central question that drives the plot. Which drives the author envy, spite, or a thirst for vengeance? Or is it something more sinister a perverted joy that comes from the ability to control another person with only a quill and some paper while causing them agony from a distance? The filmmakers dive into the darkest corners of the human psyche to examine the psychology of the poison-pen writer, exposing the various reasons why people carry out cruel and dishonest deeds. The Effect on the Grantee The consequences of receiving a poison pen letter might be disastrous for the recipient. In "Wicked Little Letters," Edith's character struggles with the consequences of the letters' arrival and is thrown into a whirlwind of uncertainty and hopelessness. Edith finds herself alone and isolated as the poison-pen writer's campaign of terror turns her once-stable world upside down. She struggles to keep her cool in the face of growing suspicion and rumors. Viewers are dragged into Edith's inner struggle as the film progresses, seeing directly the psychological toll that the poison-pen letters exact and the extent she will go to in order to find the truth. The Poison-Pen Letters Legacy Even while poison-pen letters seem to be a thing of the past, their influence is still seen in the digital age. The instruments of the poison-pen writer are now more available than ever because to social media and anonymous messaging services. The methods may have changed from cyberbullying to online harassment, but the underlying intentions are still the same: to cause harm from a distance, to sow dissension and mistrust, and to take pleasure in the mayhem that results. With "Wicked Little Letters," the filmmakers provide a poignant reminder of the poison pen letter's enduring power and the necessity of being vigilant against those who use the written word to sow discord and hatred. By examining the phenomenon of poison-pen letters, the makers of "Wicked Little Letters" have produced a complex examination of human nature and society's darkest tendencies, in addition to a story of mystery and tension. They challenge audiences to face the painful facts at the core of the poison-pen letter a phenomena that is as old as the written word itself, but is nevertheless relevant and unsettling today through painstaking attention to detail and powerful storytelling. The phenomena of the poison-pen letter is what acts as a chilling reminder of the power of words, the fragility of trust, and the evil that lies inside all of us as the story progresses and the secrets of the past are revealed.

Chapter 4.

The True Story Behind "Wicked Little Letters

In the early 1920s, amidst the tranquil countryside of Sussex, a scandal of unparalleled proportions unfolded a scandal that would come to be known as the Littlehampton Letters. It all began innocuously enough, with the arrival of a series of anonymous letters bearing shocking and obscene content. But as the missives continued to arrive, their impact rippled through the tight-knit community, leaving a trail of devastation in their wake. At the heart of the scandal were the residents of a sleepy village, whose lives were upended by the poison-pen writer's campaign of terror. The true story behind "Wicked Little Letters" is a tale of secrets, lies, and the corrosive power of gossip a cautionary reminder of the dangers of unchecked rumor and innuendo.

-The Cast of Characters:

Central to the true story behind "Wicked Little Letters" are the individuals whose lives were touched by the poison-pen writer's campaign of terror. At the center of it all was Edith, a respectable middle-aged spinster who found herself the unwitting target of the letters' malicious content. As the scandal unfolded, suspicion fell on Edith's neighbor, Rose a brash and outspoken woman whose colorful language and questionable reputation made her a prime suspect in the eyes of the townsfolk. Alongside them were a cast of supporting characters, including the county's lone female police officer, Gladys Moss, and Edith's domineering father, Edward Swan. Each character played a role in the unfolding drama, their lives intertwined in ways both unexpected and profound.

-The Mystery Unraveled:

As the true story behind "Wicked Little Letters" unfolds, viewers are drawn into a world of mystery and intrigue, where nothing is as it seems and everyone has something to hide. As the characters grapple with the fallout from the poison-pen letters and the web of suspicion and betrayal that surrounds them, the true identity of the letter writer remains tantalizingly out of reach. Yet, as the story progresses, clues begin to emerge, pointing towards a shocking revelation that threatens to tear the fabric of the community apart. Through meticulous research and attention to detail, the filmmakers of "Wicked

Little Letters" sought to capture the essence of the true events that inspired the story, crafting a narrative that is as gripping as it is unsettling.

-The Legacy of the Littlehampton Letters:

Though the scandal of the Littlehampton Letters may have faded from memory, its legacy lives on in the collective consciousness of those who remember. As "Wicked Little Letters" reminds us, the events of the past have a way of shaping the present, influencing the way we view ourselves and each other. In exploring the true story behind the film, viewers are invited to confront uncomfortable truths about human nature and society's capacity for cruelty and deceit. Yet, amid the darkness, there is also hope a belief that, by shining a light on the shadows of the past, we can learn from our mistakes and strive to create a better future.

-Conclusion:

In delving into the true story behind "Wicked Little Letters," the filmmakers have crafted more than just a tale of scandal and intrigue; they have created a portrait of a community grappling with the consequences of its actions a reminder that the past is never truly forgotten, and that the secrets we keep have a way of coming back to haunt us. As the film draws to a close, viewers are left to ponder the true meaning of the Littlehampton Letters and the enduring legacy of a scandal that continues to fascinate and disturb to this day.

Chapter 5.

Comedic Elements: Sweary Dialogue and British Comedy

Title: British Comedy and Sweary Dialogue as Comedic Elements A Comedy Overview in "Wicked Little Letters" Comedy has always been a mainstay of narrative, providing laughs and humor to enlighten, engage, and amuse audiences. In "Wicked Little Letters," the filmmakers use a range of humorous devices to inject humor and irreverence into the story. The use of profanity in the language, a staple of British comedy that heightens the sense of shock and surprise throughout, is essential to the movie's comedic sensibility. The filmmakers create a hilarious and provocative experience that invites spectators to laugh at the folly of human nature by paying close attention to language and timing. Sweary Dialogue: Testing the Limits of Words The bold decision to employ profanity in the language of "Wicked Little Letters" is what makes the movie unique from other traditional comedies. Using colorful language to communicate their frustrations and wishes, the characters of "Wicked Little Letters" relish in the art of profanity, from the prim and proper spinster who lets free with a torrent of expletives to the potty-mouthed neighbor who spares no one's sensibilities. However, the profane speech has a vital narrative function that gives the characters and their relationships more nuance and authenticity far from being superfluous. The directors stretch the bounds of language to produce a hilarious, thrilling, and edgy experience that makes spectators reevaluate their ideas about what is and isn't appropriate speech. British Comedy: An Irreverent Tradition The makers of "Wicked Little Letters" have tapped into a rich vein of humor that is both ageless and unique by referencing the British comedic traditions. British comedy has traditionally been distinguished by its irreverence and willingness to take on taboo issues with sophistication and wit, from the raucous humor of Shakespearean farce to the piercing wit of Oscar Wilde. This custom is well demonstrated in "Wicked Little Letters," as the protagonists skillfully negotiate the perilous waters of controversy and intrigue using a blend of wit, charm, and scathing sarcasm. The filmmakers craft a distinctively British comedy experience that celebrates life's absurdities and the ability of laughter to uplift even the most dire situations through deft wit and razor-sharp dialogue. Comedy's Subversive Power "Wicked Little Letters" is fundamentally a comedy of manners, a subgenre of humor that exposes the fallacies and customs of polite society. Through a striking contrast between the refined manners of 1920s England and the startlingly profane language used by the protagonists, the directors play with viewers' preconceptions about gender, class, and morality. They expose the follies of human conduct by using the subversive force of comedy, allowing audiences to laugh at society's mistakes while also realizing the more profound truths that are hidden beneath the surface. By doing this, they produce a humorous, thought-provoking, and enjoyable experience that encourages viewers to interact with the narrative on several levels. In summary In "Wicked Little Letters," British humor and foul language combine to produce a hilarious experience that is both outrageous and thought-provoking. The filmmakers create a story that is both entertaining and thought-provoking, pushing spectators to reevaluate their assumptions about language, society, and comedy itself through the subversive power of humor and deft use of language. The protagonists ask viewers to accompany them on a hilarious and fascinating adventure as they deftly and irreverently traverse the scandalous world of 1920s Sussex. The voyage is both entertaining and educational.

Chapter 6.

Character Analysis: Edith, Rose, and Supporting Characters

Title: Edith, Rose, and Supporting Characters: A Character Analysis Character Analysis Overview of "Wicked Little Letters" In "Wicked Little Letters," the characters are the central focus of the narrative, propelling it ahead through their aspirations, anxieties, and intentions. Edith and Rose, two women whose lives are entwined in the scandalous events taking on around them, are at the core of it all. Viewers are given an insight into the intricacies of human nature and the larger societal dynamics at work in Sussex in the 1920s through their eyes. The movie has a large group of supporting characters in addition to Edith and Rose, each of whom has a special part to play in the drama that is developing. The filmmakers weave a complicated web of characters with minute attention to detail and deep characterization, giving the narrative depth and complexity. Edith: The Righteous and Original Spinster When the letters with poison pens first appear in "Wicked Little Letters," Edith is portrayed as a decent middle-aged spinster whose peaceful existence is upended. Edith is prim and polite, the epitome of moderation and decorum, but underlying her calm demeanor is a fiercely determined and inner-strong woman. As the story develops, Edith is thrown into the public eye and has to gracefully and courageously face the allegations and gossip that are circulating about her. Viewers are given a moving look at vulnerability and resiliency via Edith's journey as she deals with the fallout from the terror campaign of the poison-pen writer. Rose: The Audacious Next-door In contrast to Edith's prim and polite manner, Rose is portrayed as a boisterous and talkative neighbor whose dubious reputation and colorful language make her a major suspect in the eyes of the locals. However, beyond her tough exterior is a lady of unexpected complexity and depth, whose compassion and commitment come through in trying times. As the movie progresses, Rose becomes a pivotal character in the drama that is developing, her steadfast support of Edith acting as a ray of hope in the face of hardship. Rose challenges viewers to reevaluate their assumptions about class, gender, and morality through her interactions with Edith and the other characters. She provides a welcome contrast to the stuffy norms of polite society. Complementary Personas: An Ensemble of Characters "Wicked Little Letters" has a wide range of supporting characters, each with a distinct part to play in the drama that is developing, in addition to Edith and Rose. The supporting cast, which includes Edith's controlling father Edward Swan and the lone female police officer in the county, Gladys Moss, adds nuance and complexity to the narrative by bringing to life the desires, anxieties, and motivations of the people living in 1920s Sussex. Viewers are given a complex picture of a society dealing with the fallout from its deeds as well as the continuing strength of friendship and solidarity in the face of hardship via their encounters with Edith and Rose. In summary In "Wicked Little Letters," Edith, Rose, and the other characters weave together to form a complex and nuanced personality tapestry that enhances the narrative. Viewers are given an insight into the intricacies of human character and the larger societal dynamics at work in 1920s Sussex through their interactions and relationships. The protagonists urge viewers to embark on an instructive and amusing adventure of discovery as they maneuver through the scandalous world of whispered gossip and poison-pen letters.

Chapter 7.

Social Commentary: Patriarchal Society and Repressive Norms

Title: Social Commentary: "Wicked Little Letters": Patriarchal Society and Repressive Norms. Overview The filmmakers explore the complex layers of social criticism in "Wicked Little Letters," emphasizing in especially the patriarchal society and the oppressive customs that prevailed in Sussex in the 1920s. Viewers are taken back in time to a period when gender roles were strictly defined and social expectations frequently inhibited individual expression and autonomy through the prism of this period drama. The film highlights the structural injustices and inequities present in such a society by focusing on the interactions and experiences of characters like Edith and Rose. This causes viewers to consider the pervasive legacy of patriarchal systems and the repressive nature of cultural norms. Patriarchal Culture: Authority and Domination In the patriarchal society portrayed in the movie, men have disproportionate power and influence over others, influencing their lives and fates. An excellent illustration of this patriarchal control is provided by Edith

Swan's father, Edward Swan, who rules Edith's life and choices with an iron grip. His strict adherence to gender norms and authoritarian manner are a reflection of the times in which women were expected to submit to male authority figures in all situations. Gladys Moss was treated dismissively by the male police officers, which highlights the institutional frameworks and law enforcement's widespread sexism, which serves to further solidify the patriarchal hierarchy. Edith's battles against patriarchal restrictions provide a moving commentary on the restrictions imposed on women's agency and autonomy in such a society throughout the entire movie. Her continuous attempts to fulfill her desire for independence and self-determination are blocked by commitments to her family and society, underscoring the fundamental inequity of a system that denies women equal rights and opportunities. Despite her brilliance and tenacity, Edith is confined to a patriarchal society and struggles to define herself and carve out a future for herself in the face of repressive forces. Repressive Norms: Consequences of Conformity "Wicked Little Letters" examines restrictive standards that control behavior and social relationships inside the community in addition to patriarchal authority. Social norms have a significant impact on the lives of the characters, influencing their ideas, aspirations, and behaviors. These norms might range from the strict demands of class and decorum to the oppressive restrictions of gender and sexuality. The community's wrath is sparked by the poison-pen letters, which highlight the vulnerability of social order and the extent people will go to maintain their reputations and appearances. Because Edith and Rose disobey oppressive conventions, they upend the status quo and upset the established order, which provokes criticism and retribution from those who want to keep things the same. They are viewed as outsiders and are met with criticism and scrutiny from both authorities and their peers because they refuse to live up to social norms. But their readiness to oppose oppressive standards also gives them the ability to claim their agency and their right to self-expression, which in turn encourages others to doubt the legitimacy of the established social structure. The Ability to Resist: Overcoming Anticipations "Wicked Little Letters" honors the strength of defiance and resistance in the face of persecution despite the overwhelming impact of patriarchal society and repressive standards. By refusing to be silenced or sidelined, Edith and Rose show the transformational power of individual agency and group action, encouraging others to challenge the existing quo and doubt the validity of patriarchal structures. By their acts of disobedience and resistance, they provide room for different viewpoints and narratives, upending the prevailing discourse and creating fresh opportunities for social development. In summary With "Wicked Little Letters," the filmmakers expose the injustices and inequalities that typify Sussex in the 1920s while delivering a scathing critique of patriarchal society and oppressive customs. Viewers are prompted to consider the repressive nature of social conventions and the persistent legacy of patriarchal structures through the experiences of characters such as Edith and Rose. The movie also emphasizes the transformative power of individual agency and group action in upending established power dynamics and promoting social change, celebrating the strength of resistance and defiance. Viewers are challenged to examine their own assumptions and ideas as they interact with the social commentary in the movie, which ultimately encourages them to envision a more just and equal future.

Chapter 8.

Critical Reception: Mixed Reviews and Praise for Performances

Title: Evaluations and Acclaim for "Wicked Little Letters" Performances in the Critics' Pen. Overview A movie's perception, audience expectations, and total commercial success are all greatly influenced by the critical reception it receives. "Wicked Little Letters," a movie that takes place in Sussex in the 1920s, received mixed reviews when it first came out. Reviewers had mixed feelings about different parts of the movie. This chapter explores the critical reaction of "Wicked Little Letters," looking at the elements that led to the conflicting reviews and the cast members' performances that drew praise and criticism. We can learn more about the film's merits and faults as viewed by various reviewers by examining the response. Accolades for Performances: Showcasing the Talent of Colman and Buckley The cast of "Wicked Little Letters" garnered repeated accolades from critics, especially Olivia Colman and Jessie Buckley for their performances. Recognized for her adaptability and capacity to embody nuanced roles, Colman gave a remarkable performance as Edith, the prim and proper spinster at the heart of the movie's story. The way Colman portrayed Edith's inner struggle and resiliency was praised by critics, who also praised her for deftly navigating the character's emotional journey throughout the movie. Likewise, Jessie Buckley's interpretation of Rose, Edith's bold next-door neighbor and confidante, won praise for being both genuine and nuanced. Critics and viewers alike were moved by Buckley's ability to portray Rose's complexity, from her outspoken exterior to her inner sensitivity. She was praised for her nuanced performance. One of the film's greatest strengths, according to critics, was the chemistry between Colman and Buckley. They had a tangible dynamic that gave their on-screen romance depth and genuineness. Their exchanges, which ranged from tense exchanges to friendly times, won accolades for their emotional genuineness and gripping depiction of female friendship in the face of hardship. The supporting cast of "Wicked Little Letters" received praise for their roles in the movie in addition to Colman and Buckley. Critics commended actors like Timothy Spall, Anjana Vasan, and others for their performances, pointing out that the group was able to give each character a sense of complexity and realism. From Spall's portrayal of Edith's controlling father to Vasan's portrayal of the county's only female police officer, each actor added to the diverse cast of characters who made up the universe of "Wicked Little Letters." Mixed Reviews and Criticism: Thematic Depth and Narrative Structure Some reviewers criticized "Wicked Little Letters" for certain aspects of its narrative structure and thematic depth, despite the accolades given to the actors. One frequent criticism of the movie was its pacing, with some critics pointing out that the story occasionally felt jumbled and unbalanced. Another area of dispute raised by critics was the movie's shift in tone from humorous to more serious issues. Some felt that this was abrupt and took away from the overall coherence of the narrative. Furthermore, despite the fact that the movie touched on significant issues like gender inequality and society norms, several critics thought these topics were not sufficiently developed or investigated. Some critics felt that the film missed potential to explore these themes more deeply and provide more nuanced commentary, viewing the representation of patriarchal society and restrictive customs in 1920s Sussex as shallow. In summary In conclusion, reviews of "Wicked Little Letters" were mixed, with varying opinions on the movie's merits and shortcomings. Reviews were mostly positive. Although the performances, especially Olivia Colman's and Jessie Buckley's, received high appreciation for their sincerity and emotional nuance, the movie's narrative structure and thematic development drew criticism. "Wicked Little Letters" managed to provoke discussion and controversy among critics and viewers in spite of the film's varied reviews, bringing attention to the subjective nature of film criticism and the difficulties involved in evaluating artistic works.

Conclusion

Title: Recap: "Wicked Little Letters" Is a Complex and Fun Movie Overview As we get to the end of our analysis of "Wicked Little Letters," it is clear that the movie is a complex and enjoyable depiction of life in 1920s Sussex. Throughout our examination, we have explored a number of facets of the movie, including its performances, social criticism, and critical reception. In this last chapter, we evaluate the movie's merits and contributions to the film industry as well as its long-term influence on viewers and the larger cultural context. Delicate Presentation of Characters and Ideas The subtle way that "Wicked Little Letters" portrays its topics and characters is one of its best qualities. A comprehensive examination of human nature and society dynamics is provided by the film through the characters of Edith and Rose, along with the supporting ensemble. Particularly Edith and Rose show themselves as realistic and multifaceted characters who deal with social constraints and personal issues in a patriarchal and oppressive setting. Their friendship acts as a strong narrative anchor, demonstrating the tenacity and power of female camaraderie in the face of hardship. "Wicked Little Letters" addresses significant issues including gender inequality, cultural conventions, and the power dynamics present in patriarchal countries in addition to its characters. Even if some reviewers felt that the movie should have explored these themes more, its examination nonetheless provides insightful information about the difficulties women faced in the early 20th century and the issues that still matter today. The video invites viewers to analyze the ways that gender and power impact both individual lives and society systems by shedding light on the experiences of Edith, Rose, and other characters. Joyful and Thought-Provoking "Wicked Little Letters" is an enjoyable and thought-provoking picture that excels beyond its conceptual depth. Olivia Colman, Jessie Buckley, and the supporting cast give outstanding performances that enhance the script by giving their characters nuance and realism and enthralling viewers with their poignant emotional resonance. In particular, the chemistry between Colman and Buckley gives the movie depth by bringing warmth, humor, and poignancy to their exchanges. Furthermore, "Wicked Little Letters" skillfully blends drama and humor, flitting between lighter moments and darker subjects. The movie's ability to combine humor with depth enhances its overall appeal and accessibility, although some critics pointing out that the tone swings could be startling at times. With its colorful characters, clever dialogue, and captivating story turns, 1920s Sussex captivates audiences and draws them in. Effects and Heritage "Wicked Little Letters" is having a bigger and bigger impact on culture as long as viewers continue to connect with it. Viewers are prompted to reflect on their own views and opinions regarding gender equality and social justice as a result of the film's examination of gender, power, and societal conventions. The film reminds viewers of the strides made in the battle for gender equality while also emphasizing the work that still needs to be done by focusing on the experiences of women in the early 20th century. "Wicked Little Letters" not only contributes to the theme but also creates a lasting impact with its endearing characters and performances. Particularly, Olivia Colman and Jessie Buckley's interpretations of Edith and Rose have solidified their reputations as two of the most gifted actors of their time, winning praise from both reviewers and viewers. Beyond its initial release, the movie left a lasting influence that encouraged other generations of artists and filmmakers to investigate related subjects and storylines with complexity, subtlety, and sensitivity. In summary To sum up, "Wicked Little Letters" is a complicated and enjoyable movie that provides insightful perspectives on the intricacies of society dynamics and human nature. With a blend of drama, humor, and social commentary, the film captivates spectators with its thought-provoking ideas, unforgettable performances, and engaging characters. "Wicked Little Letters" solidifies its reputation as a timeless and enduring work of art in the annals of movie history as it continues to strike a chord with audiences and provoke meaningful discussions.

Printed in Great Britain
by Amazon